HOT AIR
BALLOONS

HOT AIR BALLOONS

Ailsa Spindler

TODTRI

Dedication
For Freddie and Cameron

This book was designed and produced by
TODTRI Book Publishers
P.O. Box 572, New York, NY 10116-0572
Fax: (212) 695-6984
e-mail: todtri@mindspring.com

Printed and bound in Singapore

ISBN 1-57717-159-4

Visit us on the web!
www.todtri.com

Author: Ailsa Spindler

Publisher: Robert M. Tod
Editor: Nicolas Wright
Art Director: Ron Pickless
Typesetting & DTP: Blanc Verso UK

PICTURE CREDITS

The Bridgeman Art Library
Christie's, London: 32
Guildhall Library, Corporation of London: 20
Prado, Madrid: 15, 18/19 (painting by Antonio Canicero)
Private Collections: 6 (detail from a painting by Jean Carrau), 10, 12/13 (painting by Jean Carrau), 17, 28/29

Cameron Balloons
37 (top), 39, 44, 45, 73, 74 (top left), 74 (top right), 74 (bottom left), 74 (bottom right), 75 (top)

Mary Evans Picture Library
7, 8 (top left & right), 15, 21 (left & right), 22 (left & right), 23 (left & right), 24, 25, 26, 27 (bottom), 31, 33, 60, 61

Fortean Picture Library
Klaus Aarsleff, 9

Ronald Pearsall
8 (bottom), 11, 16, 27 (top), 30 (top & bottom), 64, 70

Picture Perfect (New York)
34, 35, 36, 37 (bottom), 38, 42/43, 50, 52/53, 66, 68/69

Ailsa Spindler
40, 41, 46, 47, 48/49, 51, 54, 55, 56/57, 58, 59, 67, 71, 76, 77, 78, 79

CONTENTS

Jean Carral

Les "enfants" s'amusent

CHAPTER ONE

THE DREAM OF FLIGHT

Opposite: Just as watching clouds and birds in flight inspired early attempts at human flight, hot air balloons continue to inspire artists with the beauty of their simple form.

Above: The classical myth of the flight of Daedalus and his son Icarus was based on the erroneous idea that human muscles could flap wings to sustain flight.

Since before recorded history, mankind has dreamed of flying through the air. Inspired by the mastery of flight made to look so simple by birds, brave souls launched themselves off cliffs and buildings, clad in a variety of wing-like structures. Greek mythology would have us believe that Daedalus succeeded in the attempt, only to have his son, Icarus, perish when the sun's heat melted the wax which secured the feathers on their wings when he soared too high as he exulted in the sensation of flight. More recently, Leonardo da Vinci designed several 'flying machines', but modern constructions based on his plans have all failed to get into the air. The basic problem encountered by all early attempts to copy the birds is the inadequacy of human muscle; our power-to-weight ratio is not enough to sustain controlled flight. Romantic writers imagined carriages hauled through the air by teams of swans, eagles or winged horses, but there is no evidence of serious attempts to harness the power of birds – they would, of course, be doomed to failure.

However, the early dreamers must have included some who watched the clouds rather than the birds. What could be simpler than floating effortlessly on the breeze, like a ship borne on the sea? It seemed that a craft could be carried on the 'surface' of the atmosphere, if only it could ascend among the clouds. The elusive lifting force, to climb into the sky, was sought

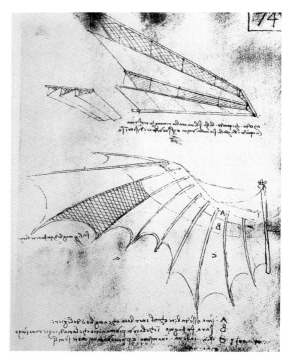

Above: The wings on Leonardo's flying machine were designed to be flapped, in the same way a bird flies. It was only when inventors stopped copying birds, and looked at the clouds and the atmosphere, that human flight became a reality.

Above: The Renaissance genius, Leonardo da Vinci, proposed several designs for flying machines.

Right: The 18th-Century French author, Decamps, was the first author to propose balloons shaped like human, or god-like, figures.

Opposite: The huge figures and designs on the Nazca Desert, Peru, are only visible from the air.

by many different civilisations. Early accounts of Chinese festivals suggest that they may have pioneered the development of small, paper balloons, like lanterns, carried aloft by smoke. Cyrano de Bergerac, the seventeenth-century French novelist, imagined a man carried upwards by flasks of dew worn on a belt, with the lifting force increasing as the sun evaporated the liquid. Pre-Inca inscriptions in Peru show possible designs for balloons, and proponents of a Peruvian claim to the first manned flight point to the presence of huge pictures on the flat Nazca plain, which only make sense when viewed from the air. There is no firm evidence that flight was anything but a dream until the scientific breakthroughs of the eighteeth century.

The eighteenth century brought the Age of Reason and the Enlightenment to

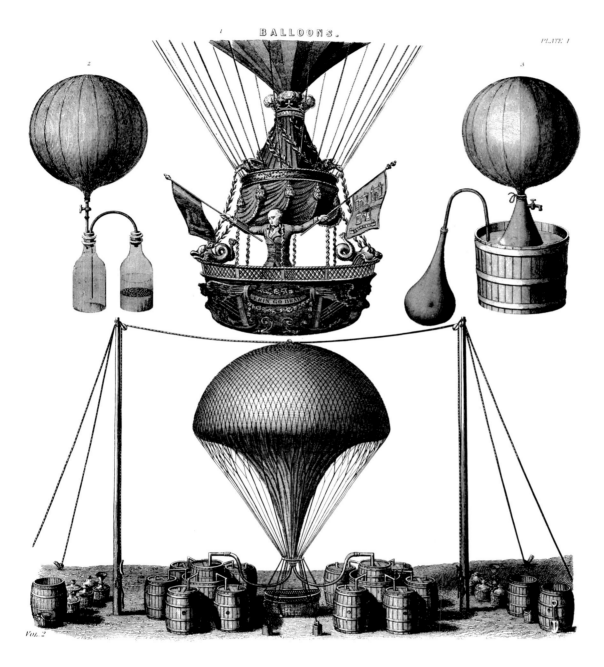

BALLOONS.

Western Europe. As well as great philosophical debate and questioning of 'divine truths', this encouraged practical experimentation in the quest for scientific understanding of the world about us. Scientists discovered new gases – now called hydrogen and oxygen – and experimented with atmospheric effects produced by the creation of a vacuum. These investigations into the nature of the atmosphere gradually revealed what was to become the technological basis for the first manned balloon flights, but the realisation of the dream of flight depended on the rivalry of two Frenchmen from quite different backgrounds, but united by that dream – Joseph Montgolfier and Jacques Charles.

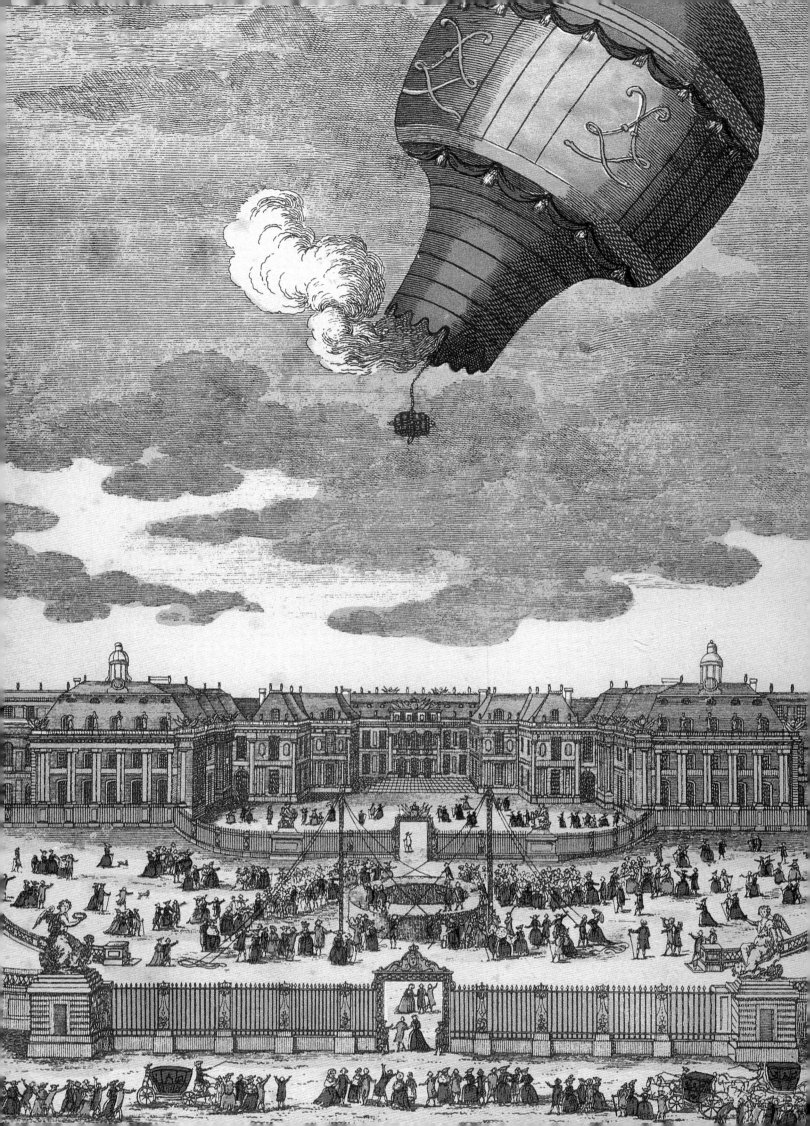

CHAPTER TWO

MONTGOLFIER BROTHERS VERSUS MONSIEUR CHARLES

Joseph Montgolfier (1740-1810) and his younger brother Etienne (1745-1799) worked in the family business, the manufacture of paper at Annonay, in south-eastern France. A well-read and intelligent man, Joseph was fascinated by flight, and began experimenting with the materials at hand in order to build a flying machine. Popular mythology has it that he was inspired by watching a piece of paper drawn up a chimney by the blazing fire below – or was it his night-shirt, or just sparks carried upward by the heat? What is not in dispute is that Joseph was familiar with Cavendish's discovery of hydrogen, and he experimented with paper bags of this 'lifting gas'. He soon discovered that the gas

easily permeated any container he could make, so he turned to investigating the potential of what he called 'rarefied air' – that is, air associated with combustion.

We now know the physics behind the lifting properties of hot air. Air expands when heated, so that it weighs less than the volume of cold air which it displaces, and is buoyed up by it. Joseph Montgolfier, like the leading scientific minds of the time, did not understand this natural phenomenon. His explanation was that the fire itself generated 'rarefied air', which was sometimes invisible but could often be seen as smoke. His experiments led him to believe that certain smoky fires produced the

greatest lift; the best fuel appeared to be a mixture of damp wool and chopped straw! The explanation for this curious finding is probably the sealing effect of the smoke particles on the fine silk fabric that Joseph Montgolfier was using. Whatever the reason, early experiments indoors were encouraging, and in November 1782 Joseph successfully inflated a small silk balloon using hot air, which flew to a height of some 70 feet. This flight was witnessed by Etienne, who was enthralled by his brother's achievement; the two men enthusiastically set about building a larger flying machine.

Further trials led to a combination of silk and paper giving the best results, and in April 1783 the brothers launched a balloon with a lifting force of some 450 lbs which climbed to 1000 feet and landed half a mile from the launch point. It was now clear to the Montgolfiers that they had designed something noteworthy, and they resolved to give a public demonstration of their invention at Annonay. A large and sceptical crowd gathered on 5th June 1783, to watch the inflation of the huge fabric structure. The difficult process of introducing heat into the flaccid envelope was completed without mishap, and the audience's sense of wonder grew as the balloon reached its full size of 110 feet

The ascent of the
GREAT MONTGOLFIER BALLOON,

Previous pages:

Far left: Joseph Montgolfier; paper-maker, scientist and inventor, this provincial Frenchman deserves the title 'Father of Flight'.

Left: Jacques Charles; scientist and balloonist. His invention of the gas balloon was prompted by rivalry between the Montgolfier brothers and the scientific intelligentsia of Paris in the Academy of Sciences, of which Charles was a member.

in circumference. Wonder turned to amazement when Joseph gave the order to release the craft, whereupon it soared silently and majestically into the air. Contemporary accounts suggest it rose to 6000 feet; certainly it flew for ten minutes before landing a mile and a half away. Etienne's explanation of the brevity of the first public balloon flight – that the 'gas' leaked out of the buttonholes where the sections of fabric were joined together – seems entirely credible!

News of this dramatic and successful display soon reached the scientists and philosophers in Paris. In danger of being upstaged by two provincial paper makers, the members of the Academy of Sciences resolved to conduct a balloon experiment of their own. Unaware of the true nature of the Montgolfiers' invention, the Academy members assumed that the lifting gas was hydrogen, and they rapidly commissioned a brilliant young physicist, Jacques

Charles, to build a hydrogen balloon.

Charles (1746-1823) enlisted the help of Ainé and Cadet Robert, who had perfected the technique of coating silk fabric with rubber to overcome the leakage problem which Jacques Montgolfier had encountered in his early trials with hydrogen. Charles' attempt was to be funded by public subscription, and the interest shown by the inhabitants of Paris soon raised the necessary funds – and guaranteed a huge audience for the launch. Indeed, such was the press of spectators at the first trial ascent, to 100 feet on a rope tether, that plans for the first free flight were changed, with the launch moved to the wide open spaces of the Champs de Mars. On 27th August 1783, the Globe (the craft's official name) proceeded to its launch point with great ceremony. The assembled throng waited patiently while full inflation was achieved, and at 5 p.m. the balloon

Opposite: Hot air balloons, or 'Montgolfières', continued to be built well into the nineteenth century, although gas balloons were quickly gaining supremacy. In 1838, J W Hoar built this massive hot air balloon, 130 feet tall and with a volume of 170,000 cubic feet - comparable with today's modern passenger-carrying giants. In fact, this balloon never flew, and the disappointed and enraged crowd who witnessed its only inflation rioted, destroying the balloon with a barrage of stones and bottles.

Right: Louis XVI, King of France, was greatly interested by the early balloon flights, and witnessed the launch of the Montgolfiers' balloon which carried aloft the sheep, cock and duck from Versailles on 17th September 1783. He and his Queen, Marie Antoinette, were eager to witness the inflation from close quarters, but were driven away by the obnoxious smoke from burning straw, wool and old shoes which were deemed the best fuel!

Above right: Joseph Montgolfier's early experiments soon attracted the attention of his brother, Etienne. After witnessing an unmanned ascent, Etienne became an enthusiastic collaborator in the quest for flight, but he never flew himself. Joseph's only flight was in le Flesselle in Lyon in 1784.

Opposite top right: The early Montgolfier designs, with their large mouth and tear-drop shape, were not dissimilar to the modern hot air balloon, whose construction uses computer-aided design to give the optimum shape

over the city skyline, the Globe flew for a total of 45 minutes and came to rest some 15 from the launch point – where it was attacked by the local peasantry, in the belief that it was some sort of devilish creature. It is easy to deride such innocence, but an illiterate country-dweller would have no idea of the strange goings-on in the nearby city. Even today, at the end of the twentieth century there are plenty of credulous people prepared to believe in UFOs rather than rational explanations.

The success of Charles' demonstration fuelled the friendly rivalry between him and the Montgolfiers and raised public interest in balloons to a frenzy. The Montgolfier brothers moved their operations to Paris, and in September they built the largest balloon ever seen to that date. Rumours that it was to carry a man aloft caused great consternation, as conventional wisdom had it the life would expire away from the ground. As a compromise, a cage was built to carry a cock, a duck and a sheep, and after several problems with bad weather this beautifully decorated craft was inflated at Versailles, in front

floated upwards, announced by a cannon shot. The crowd watched, enthralled, as the Globe climbed upwards, disappearing into cloud after two minutes, to reappear moments later to the delight of the audience. Eventually disappearing from view

of a Royal audience and with much feasting and celebration. King Louis XVI and Marie Antoinette made to approach the balloon to inspect the inflation, but used leather shoes had been added to the fire (to improve the lifting qualities of the rarefied air!) and the resulting stench drove the Royal couple to a safe distance.

The launch was greeted with the expected roars of delight and wonder, and the King declared himself satisfied with the exhibition, but Joseph Montgolfier was disappointed that the flight only lasted eight minutes – the result of two tears in the fabric during the inflation. After this brief flight, the balloon landed amongst trees, causing the cage to spring open; the first observers on the scene noted that the sheep was quietly grazing, and the duck was unharmed. There was some concern when it was found that the cock had an injured wing – perhaps a strange effect from the flight – but several observers

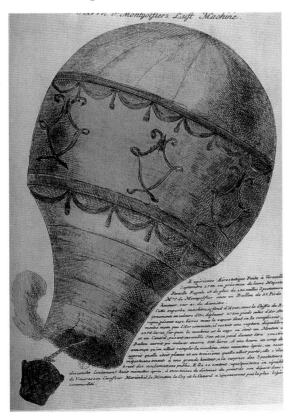

attested that the sheep had kicked the cock before take-off. Nevertheless, the safe transport of the animals had cleared the way for the first manned flight, and both the Montgolfiers and Charles proceeded to build a man-carrying device.

Above: Marie Antoinette, Louis XVI's Queen. The Royal family witnessed several early flights, and a balloon named after her flew 36 miles in 45 minutes in 1784.

23

CHAPTER THREE

THE FIRST MANNED FLIGHT

Opposite: A somewhat extravagant contemporary nineteenth-century illustration of a manned balloon flight over Paris from 100 years earlier.

Below: Pilâtre de Rozier; the first aeronaut.

The King was concerned by the possible danger to a human taking to the air, and decreed that if the next Montgolfier balloon was to demonstrate manned flight, it should carry two convicts. This decision was challenged by a young scientist, Pilâtre de Rozier, who had witnessed the safe landing of the sheep, duck and cock. Arguing that it was wrong for the glory of mankind's first flight to go to criminals, de Rozier enlisted the help of a nobleman, the Marquis d'Arlandes, to petition the King. They eventually prevailed, and were given permission to take their place in history.

The Montgolfiers, assisted by the enthusiastic de Rozier, speedily built another balloon, designed to carry the two men in safety. Several test inflations and tethered flights increased the balloon mania which had gripped Paris, and on the day of the actual ascent a "vast multitude" had gathered at the Dauphin's château in the Bois de Boulogne. After a delay caused by damage to the balloon during a gusty inflation, the first manned flight finally ascended at 1.54 p.m. on 21st November 1783. The Marquis later wrote a full account of the flight, showing de Rozier to be something of a natural pilot

Left: Early hot air
balloons tended to have
elaborately decorated
envelopes, of painted
cloth and paper.

Opposite: 21st
November 1783; the
first manned flight, in a
Montgolfier balloon.

Below: The Marquis
d'Arlandes; persuaded
King Louis of the merits
of de Rozier's argument,
that criminals did not
deserve the honour of
making the first flight.
The king's consent to de
Rozier's flight was con-
ditional on the Marquis
accompanying him.

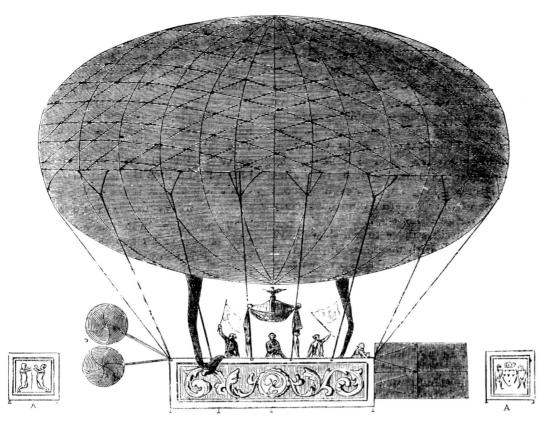

ASCENT OF A BALLOON FROM THE PARK OF ST. CLOUD, JULY 15, 1784.

in the way he managed the balloon. The two men rose over Paris, and like many a modern balloon passenger the Marquis was fascinated by the panoramic view. He cried out in excitement, naming the districts of Paris on either side of the Seine, until snapped out of his reverie by de Rozier. "If you look at the river in that fashion you will likely bathe in it soon," exclaimed the younger man. "Some fire, my dear friend, some fire!" The flight continued across the city, with both men stoking the fire with bunches of straw. At one point the Marquis was alarmed by the sight of several holes in the fabric, and several of the suspension ropes seemed to be damaged by stray flames. He expressed a wish to land, but the cool-headed de Rozier pointed out that the damage was superficial, and after applying damp sponges to the smouldering patches, the intrepid pair flew on. Finally,

27

Previous pages:

Top right: Within a few months of the first gas balloon flight, Charles was experimenting with improvements to his design, including the paddles and sails on this balloon at Dijon, 25th April 1784. Although such devices had little effect, the gas balloon was gaining in popularity over the hot air type because of the durability of the craft. Hot air balloons were quicker and easier to inflate, but usually only lasted one flight.

Right: Jean Pierre Blanchard, the first man to fly across the English Channel, was one of the early pioneers of ballooning. This design, incorporating wings and a primitive parachute, was built for a flight on 2nd March 1784, but the structure was attacked by a man wielding a sword after Blanchard refused to take him aloft.

ASCENT OF A BALLOON FROM DIJON, APRIL 25, 1784.*

they descended gently to land after 25 minutes, having covered just over five miles, mostly at quite low altitude. The Marquis jumped out of the gallery when the balloon touched down, and turned to inspect the part deflated balloon. However, the heavy canvas fabric caused the envelope to collapse very rapidly, covering de Rozier before he could move clear. Fortunately both men were uninjured and they returned to the centre of Paris as heroes, to universal acclaim. After centuries of dreaming, mankind had conquered the air and the flight had proved that humans could survive at altitude.

Meanwhile, Jacques Charles had been constructing a hydrogen balloon capable

of manned flight. Always a meticulous scientist, he drew from the results of his test models to build a gas balloon which incorporated many of the design features which were to become the standard model for all gas balloons. On 1st December he inflated his magnificent flying machine in the gardens of the Tuileries. The crowd of 400,000 represented half the population of Paris, and was probably the largest assembly of humankind that had ever been. Accompanied by Ainé Robert, Charles launched the balloon in dramatic style, climbing much faster than the Montgolfier balloon had done, and in total silence – an effect which increased the wonderment of the audience.

Charles' balloon was technically superior to the hot air version, and this was revealed during its first flight. Charles and Robert flew above Paris and out into the open countryside, outstripping a group of horsemen following them. They made a perfect landing after two hours in the air, and such was Charles' exhilaration the he decided to launch again for a solo flight. This nearly proved his undoing, as the lightly-laden balloon rocketed upwards, to some 10,000 feet, before its pilot brought it under control. Showing great skill, Charles descended to his second perfect landing of the day near the small town of Nesles.

This display of airmanship was

Above: A somewhat stylised impression of Jacques Charles' unmanned gas balloon, the Globe, which flew about 15 miles in 45 minutes after being launched in Paris on August 27th 1783 in front of a huge crowd.

31

greeted with great celebrations by the inhabitants of Paris, who recognised that the superiority of Charles' balloon had actually eclipsed the achievements of the Montgolfier flight just ten days earlier. In spite of several successful flights by hot air balloons ('Montgolfières'), they never regained their popularity compared with hydrogen balloons ('Charlières'), and seemed destined to disappear as quickly as they had jumped onto the world stage.

The balloon fever that gripped Paris rapidly spread throughout Western Europe, with 1784 seeing first flights in Italy (hydrogen gas), Scotland (hot air) and England (gas) and the first ascent by a woman. 1785 was notable for flights in Germany, Holland and Belgium and the first flight across the English Channel, but perhaps the greatest significance was the first fatal accident involving a balloon. Sadly, this was the death of Pilâtre de Rozier. On 15th June de Rozier, accompanied by Jules Romain, launched a 'combination' balloon, consisting of a spherical hydrogen balloon on top of a cylindrical

hot air section, from Boulogne. This ill-advised construction climbed slowly to around 3,000 feet before bursting into flames and plummeting to earth; both occupants were killed, and de Rozier's place in history as the first pilot was combined with the sad distinction of being a victim of the world's first aerial disaster. This accident and other mishaps did little to dampen the public enthusiasm for ballooning, while scientists saw balloons as a way of investigating the nature of the upper atmosphere.

For the next century, the gas balloon reigned supreme; daring flights became commonplace, and the balloon found a valuable role in military operations around the world. In 1903 the Wright brothers' flight at Kitty Hawk was the dawn of heavier-than-air flight, although it took the great and tragic airship disasters of the 1930s to sound the death knell of lighter-than-air flight. Throughout this period, the hot air balloon was forgotten, seeming to be just a development stage of the conquest of the air – but its time was to come again.

Above: The Wright brothers' first flight, at Kitty Hawk, North Carolina USA, on 12th December 1903, seemed to herald the end of lighter than air flight, after two hundred and twenty years in which balloons ruled the skies.

Opposite: Charles' first gas balloon flight was altogether more controlled than the flight of de Rozier and d'Arlandes just ten days before. Such was his confidence that Charles re-ascended after his first touchdown at Nesles, for a solo flight at twilight.

CHAPTER FOUR

ONWARD AND UPWARDS

Above: Soaring majestically aloft over Bloomsbury in New Jersey, USA.

Opposite: The Stars and Stripes for ever! A patriotically designed and decorated hot air balloon from the USA.

The revival of hot air balloons, 170 years after the first, historic flight by de Rozier and d'Arlandes, is due to one man – Ed Yost, an American working in Europe. Yost's company was contracted to produce gas balloons to drop leaflets over Eastern Europe as part of the Cold War. In 1953 Yost experimented with these polythene balloons, attaching a blowtorch to make a simple hot air balloon. Further tests showed that neither the fabric nor the kerosene burners were really suitable, and trials began with nylon fabric and propane burners. In 1956 Ed Yost and three partners formed Raven Industries, which continued research into man-carrying hot air balloons with funding from the US navy. The first modern hot air balloon, built of polyurethane-coated nylon and heated by a propane-powered burner, was 40 feet in diameter with a volume of 30,000 cubic feet. It made its first man-carrying free flight on 10th October 1960, at Bruning, Nebraska, USA, thereby establishing the revival of the hot air balloon as a safe form of flight.

Technical improvements quickly followed, and Yost teamed up with Don Piccard to promote hot air ballooning as a new sport. They made demonstration flights in America and Europe, and in 1963 they made the first crossing of the English Channel by hot air balloon. While Raven and Piccard balloons were being bought by new enthusiasts in Europe, another American, Tracy Barnes, was developing his own

balloons, with more effective deflation systems and better burners. Thus three manufacturers – Raven, Piccard and Barnes – established both the sport of hot air ballooning and its commercial viability.

In 1966 the formation of the British Balloon and Airship Club signalled the establishment of the sport in Britain. Soon balloons were being built in England, initially by Omega Balloons, which soon divided to become Cameron Balloons and Western Balloons. The 1970s saw other manufacturers starting up: Thunder Balloons in England and Montgolfier Moderne in France soon made their mark.

Technological development and commercial considerations have seen a few changes in hot air balloon manufacture during the 1980s and 1990s. Some names have disappeared, some companies have amalgamated, and one or two new manufacturers have arrived, but world production is still dominated by the British and the Americans, with a handful of European producers making up the balance. Cameron Balloons, in Bristol, England, currently build around 30per cent of world production, and make more aircraft per year than Boeing!

Above: An airship form Cameron Balloons, the largest manufacturer of hot air balloons in the world.

Left: Crowded skies – a seeming surfeit of hot air balloons jostling for space in a clear blue sky.

Opposite: Taking to the sky in Del Mar, California.

CHAPTER FIVE
HOW IT WORKS – EQUIPMENT

The basic principle of hot air balloon flight is very simple, although not understood by the early 'aeronauts'. An envelope of air, open to the atmosphere at the mouth, is heated so that the air expends. This expansion drives some of the hot air out of the mouth of the envelope, so that the mass of the air inside the envelope is reduced. When the reduction in mass of the hot air equals the mass (or weight) of the balloon and its load, the balloon is in equilibrium – that is, it is ready to fly. A small increase in temperature of the hot air will reduce its mass still further, and the balloon will rise.

Since the 1950s, the technology which makes this simple form of flight both safe and affordable has been refined to produce the hot air balloon as we know it today.

The element of a balloon which is most obvious to the casual observer is the envelope – the fabric part of the craft which encloses the hot air. Nearly all balloon envelopes are built of rip-stop nylon panels, sewn together to give the desired shape and patterns of colour. For added safety the envelope is built with a network of strong nylon tapes – the so-called load tapes – which carry the load and spread

it evenly across the envelope. Modern nylon, with a variety of special coatings, will produce a balloon envelope which will remain non-porous and safe to fly for at least 500 hours.

The envelope is attached to the rest of the balloon by several flying wires, of stainless steel or kevlar. The number of flying wires – from eight to 32 – is determined by the particular design of the balloon, and how many vertical segments ('gores') it has. These wires are attached to the four corners of the burner frame, which supports the burner and transfers the load in the basket to the envelope.

A modern hot air balloon burner is capable of producing huge amounts of heat – thousands of times that produced by a domestic central heating boiler – instantaneously. This is because the burner is fed by propane in its liquid form, so that it arrives at the burner jets under great pressure. The open construction of the burner allows free flow of fresh air to the combustion area, with the result that combustion rates are close to 100 per cent. The resulting flame is long, thin, almost invisible – and very hot. During inflation, the burner heats several tons of air to a temperature of around 100 degrees Celsius in a few seconds!

Suspended from the corners of the burner frame is the basket, or gondola. Although other materials have been tried, the traditional construction of woven willow and cane cannot be bettered – a point which often causes comment from first-time flyers. The basket contains the pilot, passengers and the cylinders of propane. These cylinders, of aluminium, steel or titanium construction, are firmly strapped into the corners of the basket, in a vertical position. The liquid propane is forced up the fuel hoses to the burner by its own

Above: The inflation fan, now a standard piece of balloon equipment. It is used to fill the craft with cold air before the introduction of heat via the burners.

Opposite: The precise control of the modern hot air balloon allows safe flying even when groups of balloons are close together - but pilot vigilance is essential.

Overleaf: All eyes are fixed on the flame, which can heat several tons of air to 100 degrees celsius (212 F) in just a few seconds.

Above: A balloon basket is woven in the same way as the more conventional smaller examples.

vapour pressure. Only in very cold conditions is it necessary to pressurise the tanks with an inert gas such as nitrogen.

This simple list of equipment – envelope, burner, basket, fuel tanks – comprises all one needs to fly. This is one of the secrets of the popularity of hot air ballooning as a sport; the equipment is simple, can be stored in a shed or garage, and has low operating and maintenance costs. Of course, it is possi-

ble to spend money on accessories, and most pilots acquire a collection of instruments, radios, maps and bits and bobs which make their flying more enjoyable and probably safer- but the basics of hot air flight are still quite straightforward.

There is one further piece of equipment which has become standard in ballooning – the inflation fan. In the early years of the modern revival of hot air bal-

loons, the initial cold air was introduced into the envelope by flapping the mouth until a few large bubbles were established under the fabric. A brave (or foolhardy!) crew member then stood inside the envelope, holding the fabric apart with a broom, while the pilot fired-up the burner. The jet of flame heated the cold air, while the crew member within tried to avoid joining the conflagration! This hazardous procedure was rendered unnecessary by the inflation fan, a petrol-driven fan which fills the balloon with cold air before any heat is introduced.

All of this equipment is easily carried to the launch point in a van or a small trailer, giving the pilot an huge choice of take-off sites. At 1999 prices, a pilot can buy a ready-to-fly balloon for around US$ 15,000 – a very cheap way to fly.

Above: A set of high-tec modern ballon burners.

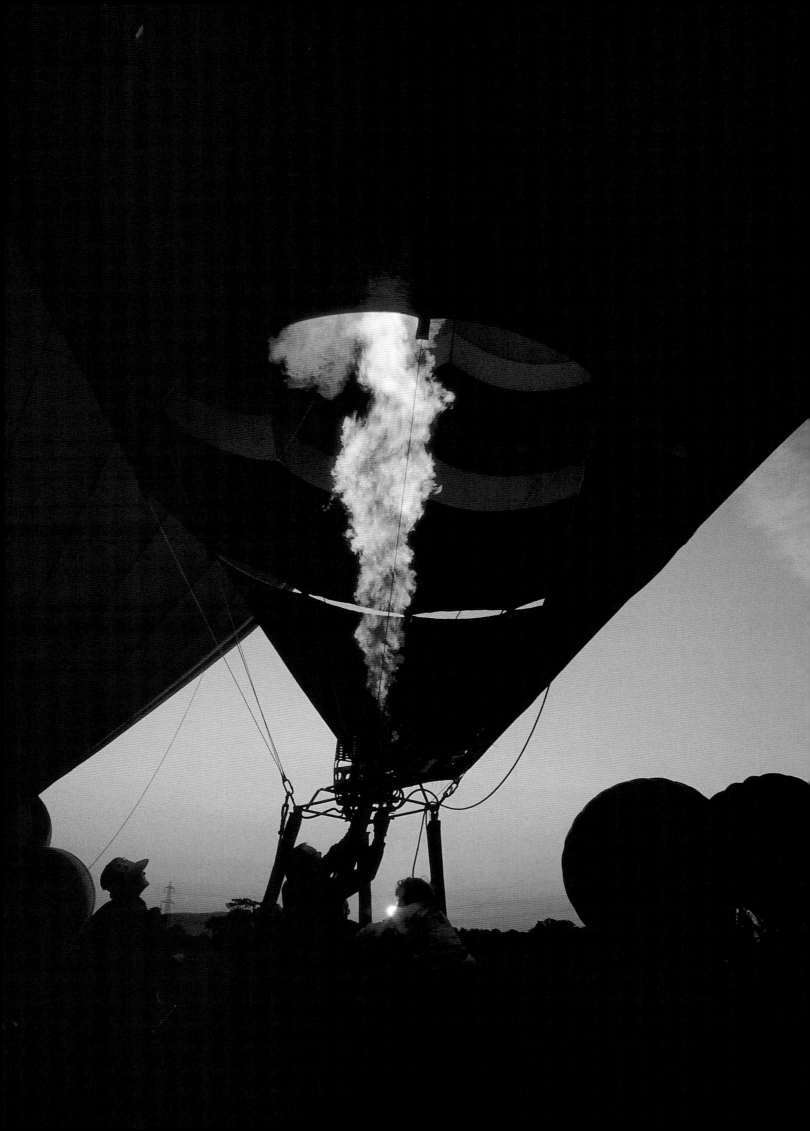

CHAPTER SIX

HOW IT WORKS – TECHNIQUES

Opposite: The tremendous power of the burner unit is what makes the modern hot air balloon so safe and controllable.

Below: A typical modern hot air balloon.

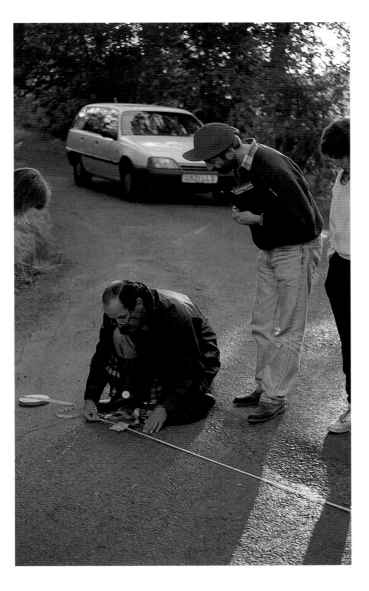

T he simple nature of the equipment may lead an observer to imagine that flying a balloon is equally simple. However, unlike most heavier-than-air craft, a hot air balloon has no automated systems to help the pilot, and flying a balloon is as close as it is possible to get to being 'at one' with the air. Indeed, many fixed-wing pilots enjoy ballooning because of the feelings of 'getting back to <u>real</u> flying'.

The pilot planning a balloon flight will have studied the weather forecast before setting out. In essence, balloons travel with the wind, so wind direction will influence the choice of launch site if downwind hazards are to be avoided. Other requirements are good visibility, gentle surface winds and a stable atmosphere; this latter prerequisite explains why most balloon flights are made in the early morning or late afternoon. During the middle of the day, solar heating of the ground warms the lower layers of the atmosphere, causing bubbles of air to rise rapidly as thermals. These thermals could cause a balloon to climb or descend violently and out of control; in the most severe cases they could rip apart a balloon.

Above: The extensive fabric of a balloon stretched out across the ground.

Opposite: Early hot air balloons normally 'landed' when their fuel ran out; today, the pilot selects a field that is suitable for landing and makes a controlled descent.

Previous pages: Ballooning is great fun. But it is also, as demonstrated here, sometimes hard work.

Having chosen the launch site, the pilot and crew assemble the balloon in a position which makes best use of any upwind shelter, and gives adequate clearance of downwind obstructions such as trees and power lines. The basket and burners are connected, with flexible rods to hold the burner clear of the top of the basket – they also prevent the burner from striking the occupants on landing. After testing that the fuel systems are functioning properly, the crew tip the basket assembly onto its side. This allows the attachment of the envelope, which is spread out downwind, and the inflation fan is moved into position near the basket. Up to this point, the preparations can be carried out in a deceptively relaxed fashion, but once inflation starts the inert

balloon swells rapidly to become more like a living creature.

With two crew members holding the mouth to allow the cold air to be blown in, and a third holding the 'crown line' – a rope which restrains the top of the envelope during the inflation process – the pilot crouches behind the burners, ready to heat the air in the envelope. Once the balloon has filled with cold air, a few seconds heating from the powerful burners causes the whole craft to lift into an upright position. First-time balloon watchers are generally surprised at the size of hot air balloons; even a 'small' sport balloon stands some 60 feet high, and the largest passenger-carrying examples are nearly twice as tall.

Left: Pilots greeting each other as they cruise close together in the skies over Oregon, USA.

Above: So, where shall we go today? Setting a course is all part of the fun and excitement of modern day ballooning.

Last minute checks on the equipment, the boarding of passengers, and a last discussion between pilot and ground crew to establish the intended flight path, then all is ready for launch. The pilot gives the passengers a briefing on what to expect during the flight, and goes through the safety procedures for the landing. When all pre-flight checks and briefings are complete, the pilot introduces a little more heat, to bring the craft to equilibrium, and releases the restraint line which prevents premature take-off. Majestically, the balloon climbs into the air and floats gently downwind. For the passengers on board the sensation is unique; there is very little feeling of movement and no wind (because the balloon moves at the same speed as the surrounding air), so it often seems that the balloon is stationary and it is the launch field that is slowly moving away!

While the passengers enjoy the amazing views of the surrounding countryside, the pilot must concentrate on flying the balloon – it will not fly itself. A little more heat to make the balloon climb to the desired altitude, then it's a matter of occasional burns to counteract the cooling of the air through the surface of the balloon. This cooling of the balloon can be used to make a controlled descent, although a vent may be opened in flight to initiate a rapid descent. Meanwhile, the pilot will be monitoring the path of the flight and

ensuring that any airspace restrictions are observed and sensitive livestock avoided – and answering a stream of 'frequently asked questions' from the passengers. A typical flight will last about an hour, so it isn't long before the pilot is thinking about landing.

Although a balloon travels with the wind, it is possible for the pilot to steer the craft to some extent. Winds vary at different altitudes, both in speed and direction, as a result of the rotation of the earth and local effects caused by the terrain. In the northern hemisphere, the wind tends to veer with altitude – 'right with height' is the rule of thumb – and the pilot will use this general principle, combined with local

knowledge, to steer the balloon towards a chosen landing field. The perfect landing field is clear of crop and livestock, has no power wires or other obstructions, and is close to a road to facilitate the retrieval of the balloon. Upwind shelter will make the landing softer by reducing the forward speed, and is something to look for if the surface wind has freshened during the course of the flight. However, the perfect field is not always available, and some landings can look like barely-controlled accidents! This is when the passengers appreciate the importance of the pre-flight briefings, and are thankful for the impact-absorbing characteristics of the wicker basket. The pilot deflates the balloon by

Above: Getting ready – preparing a balloon for its first flight of the day.

Left: From a distance, the launch field looks serene, but closer in the roar of burners, inflation fans and the scurrying crews make a balloon launch an exciting occasion.

Overleaf: Once in the air, a balloon becomes a gentle giant, floating slowly across the sky. At low levels it is possible to converse with watchers on the ground.

Left: Modern balloon fabric is nylon (or sometimes polyester), coated to reduce porosity. Available in dozens of colours, the panels of fabric are held within a network of load tapes, which bear the weight of the basket and its contents.

pulling open a vent in the top of the envelope, allowing the hot air to rush upwards, and the fabric sinks slowly to the ground like a dying beast.

Throughout the flight, the ground crew will have followed the balloon in the retrieve vehicle; their skilful navigation, perhaps aided by radio messages from the pilot, will have ensured their arrival at the landing point without too much delay, to join in the traditional celebratory drink of champagne. While the passengers reflect on a wonderful experience, the crew will pack the envelope away and load the balloon onto the vehicle, to return to base for refuelling before the next flight. Out of courtesy the pilot will try to speak to the landowner, to maintain the good relations that are an important part of good airmanship.

CHAPTER SEVEN

HIGHER, FURTHER, LONGER

Opposite: Jean Pierre Blanchard, a Frenchman, and Dr John Jeffries, an American, were the first men to fly the English Channel, on 7th January 1785. Although Jeffries paid for the flight he was nearly denied by Blanchard, who wanted all the glory for himself.

Below: The first balloon flight over England was made by an Italian, Vincenzo Lunardi, who flew a gas balloon from the grounds of the Honourable Artillery Company at Moorfields, London, on 15th September 1784.

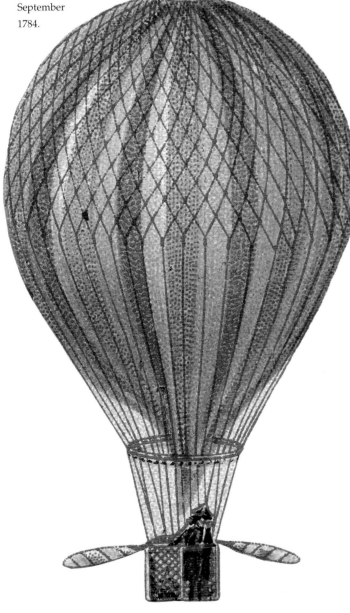

With most forms of human endeavour there is a compulsion to break records – and hot air ballooning is no exception. Indeed, one of the attractions of the sport is that there are plenty of 'firsts' waiting to be claimed, with standard equipment being quite capable of sustaining many record-breaking attempts. Most pilots will be able to find some exciting challenges quite close to home, and many national balloon associations organise challenge events to stretch the abilities of their pilots.

Many of the early 'modern' flights were records of one sort or another, by virtue of the lack of previous flights. By the mid-60s some impressive flights had been made, and 'absolute' records had been established. There are three absolute record categories: altitude, distance and duration. Such records are ratified by the Fédération Aéronautique Internationale (FAI), the regulatory body for air sports. At the end of 1966, the three absolute records for hot air balloons were:

Above: The attraction of flying over unexplored territory led to the ill-fated André expedition of 1897. A series of accidents and mishaps culminated in the deaths of three brave explorers.

Previous pages: The Swiss Alps, from 13,000ft above Chateau d'Oex; at heights above 10,000ft oxygen is recommended, although many of the pioneers of ballooning survived without oxygen at much greater altitudes.

Altitude: 28,585 feet
(Tracy Barnes, USA)

Distance: 32.6 kilometres (20.25 miles)
(Deke Sonnichsen, USA)

Duration: 1 hour 55 mins
(Deke Sonnichsen, USA)

The remarkable thing about these figures is the impressive altitude obtained, compared with modest achievements for distance and duration. This was to change, as the technology began to reach its limits during altitude record attempts but confidence in flights in fast winds grew with experience. By 1976, the absolute records were:

Altitude: 45,836 feet
(Julian Nott, Felix Pole, UK)

Distance: 542.7 kms (337.23 miles)
(Matt Wiederkehr, USA)

Duration: 18 hours 56 mins
(Don Cameron, Chris Davey, Jean Costa de Beauregard, UK)

Ten years later, the figures were:

Altitude: 55,134 feet
(Julian Nott, UK)

Distance: 1,460.7 kms (907.6 miles)
(Harold Warner, Phillip Johnson, Canada)

Duration: 40 hours 12 mins
(Hélène Dorigny, Michel Arnould, France)

In twenty years the absolute altitude record had barely doubled, while distance had increased more than 40-fold and duration more than 20-fold. The current (1999) records are as follows:

Altitude: 64,997 feet
(Per Lindstrand, UK)

Distance: 7,671.9 kms (4,767.3 miles)
(Per Lindstrand,
Richard Branson, UK)

Duration: 46 hours 15mins
(Per Lindstrand,
Richard Branson, UK)

While absolute records were being broken, other hot air flights established a variety of 'firsts'. The conquering of the English Channel in 1963 (Yost and Piccard) was followed by the first transamerican hot air flight in 1966 (Barnes). In 1977, Cameron and Yarry made the first crossing of the Swiss Alps by hot air balloon, an impressive achievement at the time but now a regular occurrence from Alpine balloon meets. Hot air balloons crossed the Irish Sea, North Sea and many other geographical barriers in subsequent years, and in 1987 Lindstrand and Branson crossed the Atlantic Ocean. Four years later, the same team conquered the Pacific Ocean, setting the current absolute distance and duration records in the process. 1991 also saw a successful flight over Mount Everest by two hot air balloons – a real test of equipment and airmanship.

The greatest challenge in any form of flight is the non-stop circumnavigation of the Earth, but it seems unlikely that this will ever be completed by hot air balloon.

The favoured type of balloon for distance attempts is the Rozière – a modern version of Pilâtre de Rozier's ill-fated combination of hot air and gas. In the modern Rozière, the lifting gas is helium, an inert gas with good lifting properties. The hot air envelope maintains the temperature (and, hence, the volume) of the helium and gives fine control of altitude. Rozières have achieved several notable flights, and in March 1999 Bertrand Piccard (Switzerland) and Brian Jones (England) successfully flew a Rozière around the globe. Their flight, in Breitling Orbiter3, took 20 days, beginning at Château d'Œx in Switzerland and finishing with a perfect landing in the desert of southern Egypt. This magnificent achievement will never be surpassed – unless someone manages to fly solo around the world in a balloon. There is a certain poignancy that the name of the first aeronaut will always be commemorated in the name of the type of balloon which successfully circled the globe.

For the less adventurous, there are plenty of other 'firsts' to be achieved in a hot air balloon. Bodies of water, ranges of mountains, even a few countries that have not witnessed a hot air balloon flight. I myself claim a couple of 'records' – the first hot air crossing of the Equator (March 1993) and the highest tethered flight in a hot air balloon (525 feet) – unless you know better!

The satisfaction of flying a balloon where no-one has flown before cannot be overestimated – especially when the successful flight is the culmination of careful planning and involves testing one's airmanship to the limit.

CHAPTER EIGHT

COMPETITION FLYING

Opposite: A balloon festival is one of the most spectacular events in the sporting calendar.

Below: The sight of balloons drifting across the countryside has inspired many people to take up this gentle sport.

The urge to compete may not manifest itself in a desire to break records. More commonly, pilots wish to test their flying skills against the skills of others in direct competition. The first US hot air balloon championship was held as early as 1963; there are now many national and international competitions sanctioned by the Commission Internationale d'Aérostation (CIA – the ballooning division of the FAI). World Championships have been held biennially since 1973; the early domination of the title 'World Champion' by American pilots has recently been successfully challenged by the top European pilots, and competition ballooning is a truly international sport.

Non-balloonists are often perplexed by the notion of competition ballooning. How, they ask, can pilots compete when they are all just carried along by the wind? It is often assumed that the pilots race each other, in the manner of yacht racing, but in fact competition ballooning is a test of flying accuracy. Each pilot attempts to reach a target, using the variation in wind with altitude to steer towards the desired point. The ability to hold the balloon at a precise level , combined with an understanding of the invisible vagaries of the breeze, are the keys to success, and require great concentration to be applied effectively. The pilot marks the exact position of the balloon in relation to the target by dropping a marker – a small bag

Above: The Gordon
Bennett Balloon Race,
for gas balloons, began
in Paris in 1906. The
venue each year is
determined by the
nationality of the previ-
ous year's winners.

Previous pages: A truly
breathtaking sight –
a row of brightly deco-
rated balloons.

weighted with sand and carrying a long nylon streamer to make it visible.

To give variety and increase the difficulty for the pilots, competition flying includes several different tasks, each with its own set of complicated rules. As well as testing flying ability, these tasks penalise pilots who do not understand the subtleties of the rules or who ignore task rules in an attempt to reach the target. Perhaps the simplest task for the observer to understand is the *Judge Declared Goal*. The Competition Director sets a common goal, to which all pilots attempt to fly from a common launch point. The goal may be a target (such as a large cross or bull's-eye), or it may be the centre of a road junction, defined by a map reference. The individual pilot has the benefit of watching the track of balloons approaching the target before deciding on the best line of approach, and

results on this type of task are often very accurate – a few inches from the centre of the target after a flight of several miles. *The Pilot Declared Goal* is similar, except that each pilot selects their own goal before take-off. This sounds easier than the *Judge Declared Goal*, but each pilot is unaware of the others' goals, so there is less advantage to be gained from watching other balloons. Other popular tasks include the *Fly In*, where pilots chose their own launch point (within limits) and fly towards a common goal; the *Fly On*, where the pilot declares a goal by writing it on the marker dropped at a previous goal; and the *Hare and Hounds*, where a non-competing balloon (the Hare) launches before the 'pack', carrying a target which is laid out when the Hare lands. These, and other more complicated tasks which may involve limited scoring areas, may be set in combination on the

same flight – for example, a *Judge Declared Goal* may be combined with a *Pilot Declared Goal* and a *Fly On*. Not all tasks involve flying to a target; the Elbow requires each pilot to attempt to achieve the maximum possible change in direction during the flight. There is even a task called *Race to a Line* – the only task that is a genuine race – but it is seldom set as it is difficult to measure the scores accurately. Whatever tasks are set, the pilot has to fly the balloon safely, read the winds, obey the rules, steer towards the target, read the map, remember which colour of marker applies to which target…and all the time watch the other balloons in the competition. Such competition flights are a true test of airmanship; occasionally luck may play a part, but the top pilots regularly fill the top positions at major championships, showing that skill and experience are being measured.

As well as the pilots and crews, competition ballooning involves a team of observers, who measure the results of the marker drops and watch out for rule infractions; the Competition Director sets the tasks for each flight; and a team of officials debrief the observers at the end of each flight, and generally assist the Director throughout the competition. Many of these associated roles attract people who have no wish to become pilots, regarding the organisation of the competition as a rewarding pastime in its own right.

Although not a physical sport in an athletic sense, a balloon competition may involve a week of getting up before dawn, flying and refuelling twice each day, and getting to bed around midnight each night. This is physically and mentally exhausting for everyone involved, and gives the lie to those who claim that competition ballooning is not a 'real' sport.

A snow covered landscape makes provides a contrasting backcloth to a flight of hot air balloons.

Oppsite: Modern technology allows balloons to be built in many different shapes - indeed, imagination seems to be the main limiting factor!

Below: Mickey Mouse takes to the air.

CHAPTER NINE
SPECIAL SHAPES

in strange shapes took some time to become established. The first special shape to fly was *Golly*, built in the mid-70s to promote a brand of jams in Britain. A simple figure, the head was a conventional balloon, with an extended 'skirt' forming the torso and legs. Two air-filled tubes represented the figure's arms, giving a convincing representation of the brand's trademark. Crowds loved *Golly* and its success prompted other advertisng shapes. A light bulb and a spark plug in Britain, a pair of jeans in Holland, and a whale in America were early examples of unusual shapes. Since then, increasing experience in manufacture and computer-aided design have led to an amazing variety of shapes: bottles and cans, buildings, vehicles, cartoon characters, shopping trolleys, motorbikes, electricity pylons and many, many more have flown, providing much entertainment and giving promotions experts undreamed-of photo opportunities. Although mostly designed for advertising purposes, a few shapes have been built "just for fun". The late Malcolm Forbes, a multi-millionaire publisher, was a special shape enthusiast, commissioning such wondrous shapes as the Taj Mahal, a Turkish sultan, a macaw, and a copy of his own French château at Balleroy. Another notable private special shape is *Pipy*, a 165 feet tall Scottish pipe major, complete with full highland regalia and a set of bagpipes. Pipy's owner, Muir Moffat, had the balloon built to celebrate his

At any large gathering of balloons, the loudest cheers from the crowd will be prompted by the launch of the Special Shapes. These extraordinary aircraft come in a huge variety of shapes and sizes, many of which seem incapable of flight.

Although gas-filled special shapes had been used for many years, to promote commercial brands and products, the idea of building hot air balloons

73

Above left: Special
shape balloons, such as
this straberry make
ideal advertising
vehicles.

Above right: Character
merchandising is used
to the full, as Sonic the
Hedgehog shows here.

Bottom left: Rupert
Bear, one of the most
enduring children's
characters.

Bottom right: Bertie
Bassett, a giant
liquorice allsort

Above: A giant Action Man making a spectacular entrance amrked with a plume of orange smoke.

pride in Scotland, and it is in great demand by gatherings of ex-patriate Scots around the world.

There is really no limit to the shapes that can be designed as free-flying hot air balloons, as long as the shape has enough mass to lift the balloon and pilot. The flying characteristics of shapes can be difficult to predict at the design stage, and many pilots have been unpleasantly surprised by the rapid climb rates of tall, thin shapes such as bottles. The more complicated the shape, the heavier the envelope will be, as it will include lots of internal partitions to maintain the desired form against the natural tendency of the fabric to take up a spherical shape. Indeed, some of the larger shapes are so heavy that they can only carry a solo pilot, and this may be the limiting factor in future designs.

Left: Two more highly unusual and inovative special shape balloons.

75

CHAPTER TEN

HOW TO BECOME A PILOT

Opposite: Even in the heat of competition, most balloon launches are a serene moment. the pilot leaves behind the urgency of the preparations on the ground, and takes a few moments to contemplate the flight ahead.

Below: Get set! Get ready! Go!

As a hot air balloon drifts serenely across the sky, it attracts many envious looks from people on the ground. Motorists may pull over to stare; excited children wave and shout greetings; and, on most flights, one or two enthusiasts will stop what they were doing and follow the balloon until it lands. For these observers on the ground, a balloon seems to belong to another world and those lucky enough to be on board seem like a race apart. This can lead people to imagine that ballooning is an exclusive sport, the preserve of the wealthy and not for mere mortals. In fact, nothing could be further from the truth. Because every pilot needs a crew to help with the launch and to retrieve the balloon at the end of the flight, volunteers are normally very welcome

In most parts of the world it is possible to buy a flight from a local commercial balloon operator. This will confirm whether or not an individual really has caught the 'ballooning bug', but it is an expensive treat and not the best way to become a regular balloonist. Far better to volunteer one's services for crewing duties, on the understanding that every so often a space will be made available in the basket. This is how most people start ballooning, with the benefit of ensuring that they get a firm grounding in all of the techniques required to crew properly. Many enthusiasts never feel the need to progress beyond this point, happy to be valued, expert crew who may be invited to exotic balloon meets all around the world.

However, most keen balloonists eventually decide that they wish to get their Private Pilot's Licence (Balloons), a permit to enjoy the freedom of

Above: Competition flights may involve everyone launching together, as here, or each pilot selecting a launch site. In either case the contest involves flying to certain pre-determined targets. A good pilot will be within a metre or two after a flight of several miles.

the skies. Requirements for this privilege vary from country to country, but generally specify a minimum number of training flights, a basic test of medical health, and written examinations which include air law, navigation and airmanship. The training schedule may be run by the national aviation authority, or delegated to the national balloon federation; either body will supply details of the examination syllabus and training arrangements for their own country.

It is possible for the trainee pilot to sign up for an 'all-in' course at a commercial ballooning school. These are generally set up in parts of the world with stable climatic conditions, and it is possible for a keen student to gain a balloon licence in a week. The main drawback with this type of instruction is that the new pilot will almost certainly have trained on just one type of balloon, in ideal weather conditions. It is important that any new pilot

continues to learn after getting a licence, but this is particularly true of the graduates of balloon schools.

Clutching a new licence, the pilot will be looking to acquire a balloon, to get plenty of flying hours logged as soon as possible. Balloon manufacturers' representatives will be keen to extol the virtues of their own products, complete with as many 'accessories' as possible. However, the new pilot should consider second-hand equipment as well. Baskets and burners are resilient, and well cared for examples should last for many years; these can be a good buy for a pilot on a restricted budget. Used envelopes lose value quite quickly, as the fabric has a limited flying life, but a balloon with up to 200 hours in the logbook should still fly as economically as a new envelope. Inexperienced pilots often cause minor burn damage around the mouth of the balloon, and it may be good sense to accept

that this may happen and buy a used envelope on which to build flying hours.

Having bought the equipment needed to get airborne, our new pilot will need to organise transportation for the kit. The choice is between a trailer (popular in Europe) or a pick-up truck (favoured in America). A trailer can be pulled by the family saloon – huge off-road vehicles are not a necessity – and they can double as covered storage in damp climates. Pick-up trucks are easier to manoeuvre and can be 'dedicated' to ballooning, with fixed radio installations and peripheral items of kit left on the vehicle. Each choice has its devotees, and the final decision will be a personal one.

There is little paperwork involved in ballooning, but most pilots carry third party and passenger liability insurance. For the infrequent flyer, the annual insurance premium may be the biggest running cost of operating a balloon. Other regular

requirements will include some sort of annual inspection of airworthiness, keeping maps up-to-date, and periodic medical checks. Providing these are in order, our new pilot is free to take to the air at last.

It is worth stressing that a good pilot never stops learning, particularly the pilot of a hot air balloon. Every balloon flight is different to those preceding it – a new launch site, perhaps; certainly different weather and a new landing field. The absence of a flight controller on the ground and the lack of complicated instruments in the basket means that the pilot depends on personal skills alone, and aeronauts with thousands of hours in the air can still encounter new situations and testing conditions. Whereas the pilot of a light aircraft may get bored with flying 'circuits' to maintain licence validity, balloonists are constantly stimulated by the changing environment in which they fly. Bored in a balloon? Never!

Above: There can be few sights more inspiring than a group of balloons flying together.

INDEX